Gift of Happiness

How to Bring More Happiness into Your Life

Table of Contents

Introduction

Why Happiness is Everything

Happiness can be likened to electricity, which powers equipment, appliances, gadgets, etc. Without this power, there is absolutely no use for electrical equipment. Imagine New York City without electrical power - everything will be at a standstill with no trains running, offices being shut down, no computers, etc. The streets will be absolutely dark and there will be no illuminated buildings and no nightlife. **Without electricity, the city is dead**.

Humans are motivated and stimulated to keep moving forward through our search for fulfillment and happiness. The city works the same way, using electricity for motivation and stimulation to function and expand. Therefore, **like electricity for the city, happiness for us humans is everything**.

We have written this book to tell you the **real secret** to finding happiness, and to show you that you can have happiness NOW, not later or tomorrow. And we promise you, it will not be something that will elude you.

Yes, happiness will be yours, only if you know how to **find it and treasure it**. You see, happiness is like a commodity; it is something that every person in this planet can possess. We could compare it to a rare gem; but just like diamonds and rubies and any other precious stone, happiness ought to be mined. In other words, you've got to search for it inside yourself, and hold onto it like the precious stone that it is.

We want to thank you and congratulate you for downloading this book, "Gift of Happiness: How to Bring More Happiness into Your Life". This book will **revolutionize the way you think** and the way you live, which will contribute and translate into experiencing true happiness. Read on and be one of the many individuals who found the "Gift of Happiness."

information is without contract or any type of guarantee assurance.

The trademarks that are used are without any consent, and the publication of the trademark is without permission or backing by the trademark owner. All trademarks and brands within this book are for clarifying purposes only and are the owned by the owners themselves, not affiliated with this document.

Chapter 1:
The Quest for Happiness

If happiness were a commodity, it would be the most expensive, most in demand item in the entire world – probably more saleable than any products there are. It would perhaps surpass rubies, diamonds, gold and other precious stones and metals in terms of value.

And if happiness were only an app that is readily available and downloadable, it would have been accessed and utilized by 7 billion people on the planet on a regular basis, perhaps every hour or every second. Unfortunately, happiness seems so distant to many.

What is Happiness? How does one get it? Let's dissect this word so we understand what it really is.

Happiness Defined

Many people have defined and explained happiness in more ways than one. Webster online dictionary, for example, defines it as "a state of well-being and contentment" and equates it with joy. Happiness is "a pleasurable or satisfying experience."

The common description of happiness is that of "a fleeting feeling of euphoria, pleasure, satisfaction or good fortune." In other words, it is a momentary gratification; it does not last. This feeling has to be sought all the time to experience fulfillment. Others have referred to happiness as a good fortune or prosperity. It is also associated with finding a true love, of marriage, and family. When a man says to woman, "you are my happiness," that speaks volumes, but for the most part, he means that the latter is his joy, his completeness, someone that keeps him energized, ecstatic, and inspired. Therefore, the word happiness also means inspiration.

Blogger and filmmaker Andrew Shapter has asked people how they understood happiness and he received numerous responses. A closer look at those responses revealed six prevailing themes - things that relate to or that result to happiness, and these are enumerated below:

a. Possession of material things

b. Engaging in meaningful activities

c. Acceptance from others and loved ones

d. A sense of belongingness

e. Making a difference and citizenship

f. Celebration

g. Freedom of Choice

These responses tell us that possessions and activities determine or give us happiness. Relationships and love are also sources of happiness and so are altruism and enjoying what there is in life. We think the idea of celebration and choosing to experience elation really stand out and make a lot of sense.

We like the description given by certain Hari P. who said that happiness is tantamount to "springs of positive feeling which is waiting to burst out from your heart." One reader thought happiness is enjoying unconditional love while yet another reader believed happiness is "finding your inner strength, and knowing it will always, always see you through any difficulties in life."

Although we agree with all the ideas as to what constitute happiness, we like what Brandy T. stated, that happiness is "in all of us." But we love these words of Jerold T. the most: "Happiness is possible. Choose to make it happen."

These are all good definitions; however, it is important to realize that happiness is more than just what others do to us; happiness is finding your own place under the sun and having reasons to live. In short, happiness is having or finding true meaning.

Chapter 2:
The Beauty of Living in the Moment

Misguided focus is a major problem among many. No, we're not talking about the inability to concentrate on what is important. We are talking about having a mind that is littered with so many concerns that we literally live in chaos. Misguided focus is a result of too many commitments. Calendars are crammed with appointments that we rarely have the chance to enjoy the present. Accomplishing what has been calendared, though that is good, becomes the only or central goal and all other things are eliminated or set aside. We need to learn to live in the moment.

Some people have what we would call a *'living for the next'* lifestyle. Next appointment, next event, next activity. When they wake up, they think of their targets for the day and allow themselves to be ruled and controlled by deadlines. While eating breakfast, they look at the computer screen to prepare some stuff for the day's events. And while showering, they try to rush so that they make it in time for their appointments. While on the road, they keep thinking of what to say in an office presentation. And while taking their lunch break, they're in a chat with business prospects and possible networks of contacts or busy fidgeting with their phone, texting or calling. No time to breathe, or to relax. They don't live for the moment but for tomorrow. As a result, they are depriving themselves of rest, of peace, of enjoyment with the now.

Sometimes, we forget to savor the aroma of a freshly brewed coffee. We eat our breakfast in a rush and don't remember how the toast tasted after eating. Suddenly, eating, drinking, showering and driving have become tasks as well. We have turned ourselves into robots, into workers, not humans who should enjoy the present and be happy with each activity of life.

You want to be happy? Enjoy your breakfast – take time to sip your hot cappuccino or tea. See what you're really eating. Let the steaming hot shower refresh you and relieve your aching muscles. Consider the bath time as your reward, a time of pampering. Enjoy the scrubbing, listen to the rhythm of the splashing water, and smell the fragrance of the soap.

While driving, listen to your favorite music, or take time to free your mind of any worries and concerns. Just enjoy the ride and be happy because you have work, you can drive, and can go anywhere you want. What a freedom! Now we don't see any reason why you would still be unhappy.

The key is enjoying what is now, without necessarily forgetting what is planned for the future. The point is to not deprive yourself of the present because as Master Shifu of the movie 'Kung Fu Panda' has aptly said, "Yesterday is history, tomorrow is a mystery, but today is a gift...that's why it's called 'present'."

If your favorite song is playing, take time to enjoy the beat and savor the message. Recall what has made it your favorite – maybe because it reflects your own aspirations, dreams, or even frustrations, or that it captured what you always wanted to articulate or the feelings that you felt once.

When being embraced by the breeze, take pleasure in it. It's free and it's yours for the taking.

As you happen to see the setting sun, pause and gaze at the golden star slowly disappearing into the horizon and observe the orange and bright rays.

If it's evening time and you're relaxing in your verandah, watch the twinkling of the millions and millions of stars that are littered in the sky. Imagine how far away they are and admire their beautiful light.

Take time to listen to the cries of your baby or the words of your grown up child, and attend to them, not as an obligation but as something that you want to do.

Take time to hug your spouse. Say many times "I love you" in your talks. Today will never come back so enjoy all the things you can for today.

Chapter 3:
Happiness Within Us

Happiness is a matter of choice. While it definitely is something that comes randomly and unexpectedly, we have a significant part in making it happen. In short, a big part of feeling or having happiness lies in your own hands.

A story is told of a naughty young boy who tested the wits of an elderly woman in India who was well known for her wisdom. She never hesitated in giving the right answers and offering the best advice. But the boy apparently was not convinced, so he went to see the old lady with a challenging test. Holding a bird in his hand behind his back, he asked the sage to tell him if the fowl was alive or dead. The woman thought for a moment. If she said the bird was alive the lad would simply press the neck of the bird and present to her a lifeless avian, so the woman reasoned. If the old villager said the bird was dead, the chap would do nothing to the bird and show a flapping fowl. Her answer surprised the boy. She said something to this effect, "Young man, I will not tell you whether the bird is alive or dead. I do not have the answer. The answer lies in your hands," she aptly said.

We are all like the boy in the story. In our hands, we hold a bird and it is up to us to decide whether it is going to be alive or dead. In the same way, it is our decision whether we would be happy or not.

What is essential is that you do all you can to experience happiness. Again, happiness is a choice; it's something that we must act upon. So what do we do to live a happy life? The answer is in your hands. In short, begin inside of you. But how?

You Can Be Happy

First, you must recognize that **you are** capable of experiencing tremendous joy, fulfillment, and happiness. It's like a switch that you have to turn on and never switch it off. The problem with some people is that they don't even know that there is a switch; or even worse, they are unaware that there's light.

There is a story of a hotel guest who stayed in his suite without light. The problem was not that the hotel had problematic lighting, the reason was that he could not locate the switch, and assumed that there must have been some problem. He was too embarrassed to ask the concierge where the switch was or what was wrong. It turned out that the guest is supposed to slip the room key, a plastic card, into the room key holder, and voila, you have a lighted room. You see, it was not the lack of light that caused the absence of brightness, but the failure of the guest to ask - to act.

Achieving happiness and fulfillment is more than just positive thinking, although that helps. It's the determination and recognition of the fact that you have the capacity to rejoice regardless of your circumstances.

Looking for the Happy Factors

Happiness seems elusive for many, and the consequences are enormous. People from all walks of life – the famous included – would rather die than live without it. Various celebrities - from the music industry to film to sports - have resorted to suicide because happiness was simply absent in their lives. They convinced themselves that they were hopeless and in no way would be able to live a happy life. But we must be very clear on this point; they were mistaken.

All those famous people had money and lived glamourous lives, enjoyed tremendous fame, and they had family to love and support them. But it seems nothing and no one gave these men and women the happiness they so longed for deep down inside. Had they known that happiness was more than just a feeling, we would not have lost another great performer, entrepreneur or innovator.

The reason why you're reading this book is because you too are longing to be happy. There are circumstances that keep crowding around you and overwhelming you, thus affecting your levels of presence or happiness. You're carrying some burdens, you're facing great challenges, and you feel you've reached the end of the road. My friends, there is no such thing as reaching the end of the road. Drivers like us know this fact. Isn't it that every time we reach a dead end, we turn the car around and find another route? You're getting our point, right?

What are we are saying here? Happiness is a **choice**. It's something that we all must seek and acquire, and we dare not stop until we have it, for it is what keeps us going. Happiness is the driving force than pushes humanity forward, while of course being a product of love.

In the rest of this book you will find a wealth of information that will not only revolutionize the way you look at happiness, but the way you look at life in general.

Chapter 4:
Uncovering the Happiness Factors

Famous 20th century psychiatrist and psychotherapist Carl Jung was once asked about what he considered to be the secrets to experiencing true happiness. He mentioned five factors and these are: physical and mental wellness, good personal and intimate relationships with loved ones and others (these include marriage, family and friends), the ability to perceive beauty and nature, acceptable standards of living and being gainfully employed, and spirituality or involvement in some religion.

We would like to give Jung some credit for these helpful thoughts. It's true that when one is healthy he or she is quite happy because nothing restrains them. They are free to do whatever they find pleasurable, thus the feeling of happiness. For example, if a person likes playing certain sports and get to engage in it on a regular basis, that becomes a source of happiness. Confine that person at home and he or she will be unhappy.

Jung's second happiness factor is true as well. Psychologists, sociologists, marriage counselors, health experts, and religious leaders all agree that people draw strength and a sense of completeness, acceptance and belonging from those they are related to or whom they love.

Similarly, people with a comfortable life and those that have satisfactory work are not or are less problematic, and so they feel good inside because there is little to cause them anxiety.

In addition, being able to enjoy the world around you is a source of positive feelings and so is religion. As we will discuss later in more detail, religious people tend to be much happier than those who have no religion at all.

Jung, however, does not give us a complete picture and we disagree with him in some respects. For example, we all know of some people who are sick or handicapped but they are happy. One can be deprived of health, resources, and jobs but still they find time to smile. For them the deprivations are a fact of life and life goes on. We also know that many unmarried people like Catholic nuns and monks, who live in poverty and whose preoccupation is only to serve others and find themselves, are oozing with lots of happy feelings! They do not have any romantic partner, they might live away from close friends, and are confined in an isolated monastery. Take for instance the sense of peace that Buddhist monks exude. They, too, live a life devoid of riches, some are unmarried, but they are at peace. We also differ with Jung on one other aspect - the connection between happiness and having the faculty to perceive beauty and nature. We all probably have met blind people whose smiles are infectious and as innocent as those of young children, and when they speak, it's as if they can see the things around them. They can only feel the cool breeze or hear the rustling leaves, or the gushing waterfalls, but they are not able to fully appreciate nature they way most people do because of blindness. Yet, they are happy!

This leads us to a very important point- you are yet to uncover the real secrets of experiencing happiness. What psychologists offer is good, but this book has even **more** - the real secrets of happiness.

Chapter 5:
Secrets of Happiness

You must know that it's your call to make yourself happy, not the world around you. Although the external world can aid in experiencing positive feelings but they are not the key. You hold the key, remember? Take the initiative. Make an action! Begin looking for all the things that can make happiness a reality.

Happiness is not a means, it's an end. It's a result of what you do and think. And bear this in mind, never let circumstances confine you. Learn to live above circumstances. How? The key is celebration.

Note that to celebrate requires an action. It's a choice. It's something that must be done only by you. When was the last time you paused and took time to celebrate? Many people are unhappy because they fail to see the beauty of life and their surroundings. The problem has a lot to do with their failure to enjoy what is.

What about you? Do you celebrate the 'here and now'? Do you choose to enjoy life? Or are you caught up in the rat race, simply living to exist and perform tasks?

You're more than just an employee, a boss, a student, a mom, a father, a sibling. You're a human being, a cause for celebration.

Celebrating Everything

We all need to learn to focus on what we have been endowed with both material and non-material, things seen and abstract. All of these are a cause for celebration. Life is a major reason to celebrate. Aren't you glad you're alive and free, meanwhile so many are stuck in war-torn countries or poverty-stricken areas?

Let's celebrate time because we have 24 hours of it in a day 365 days in a year. We have the opportunity to be expressive, to pursue our passions, spend time with family and friends, change the world and do all the other things we love because of the gift of time.

Things do not need to be extraordinary all the time. Even the mundane can bring us pockets of positive feelings and they are enough cause for celebration. You can find beauty all around you, and transform things which can seem mundane into something of extraordinary value – it's all up to you how you choose to view the world.

Learn to celebrate nature. It has so much to offer, which many often ignore. A stroll through the park, a walk by the beach, watching sunsets, feeling the cool breeze, marveling at a waterfalls, gazing at the millions of stars, playing with the fishes while snorkeling, feeding birds, and so much more.

Don't be afraid of inactivity either. Nor of silence. Enjoy "me" time by not doing anything. Don't feel guilty laying around for a while, enjoying your soft and comfy sofa or wrapped in your warm blanket.

Celebrate Belongingness

Be glad you have a spouse, or children, or grandchildren, or other relatives. Rejoice because you have at least one friend! So many people feel lonely, meanwhile our lives are surrounded with people – even strangers in the street!

You have a community of people at work, or where you travel often such as an exercise facility or supermarket. You have a faith community wherein you can feel loved, accepted, and often encouraged. Your community members visit you when you're sick or lift you up when you're down.

Many of these people share your joys and laughter. They offer advice. They cheer you up. They give a pat on the back. They tell you positive words. They believe in you.

Belonging is calls for celebration. You see, you have a home, you have a family, everywhere, every time. You will never be alone.

Celebrate Your Material Blessings

The most miserable person in the world is one that is never content with what he or she possesses. Begin inside your home – you have a room to sleep in when millions are homeless and living on sidewalks. You have a sofa and bed when others have only cardboard. You have a refrigerator and oven while others don't even know what a home cooked meal is like. You have an air conditioning unit or a heater while many others either endure extreme temperatures. Your closet is full of clothes while others may wear the same thing for years.

Celebrate Spirituality

The connection to our source is the greatest treasure. Some people would rather not have anything to do with spirituality or religion, maybe because of fear or lack of experience. Some are turned away because it doesn't grant them instant gratification or because they are opposed to the discipline of certain belief systems.

Science, particularly the field of medicine, credits religion and spirituality for cures of diseases and many other health benefits which will be discussed extensively later in this book.

Maintaining spirituality is healthy. Involvement in religious practice fills a void inside of a person that cannot be filled by anything else. This is because the understanding of our source and the platform of creation allows us to understand ourselves and the nature of the world better.

It's undeniable that going to a place of gathering, meeting new members of your faith community, spending time together are all a manifestation of dependence on the transcendence.

People try everything to achieve fulfillment – they turn to material pursuits like cars, jewelry, houses, sex, etc. But to no avail. Taking Karl Marx's comment that "religion is opium of the masses" in a more positive light, spirituality indeed gives a person not a feeling of numbness, but an ability to hold on tightly at the end of the rope. This is called faith. Just like hope, faith allows us to keep believing and moving on even when others have given up. This is a form of celebration, as well as a form of happiness, regardless of the situation.

Chapter 6:
Why Happiness is Healthy

Happiness is directly linked to gratitude. When one is grateful, everything around him or her is appreciated and beautiful. As a result, they are happy. Happiness not only makes us feel good but also keeps us healthy.

Physical Benefits

Experts tell us that happiness boosts our immune system because when we laugh, we are not stressed and we are not worried. When a person worries, his bodily functions are affected, including blood circulation, digestion, and heart rate. When we are grateful and happy, the body is more at rest and relaxed, and so its functions are not affected.

Happy people tend to take better care of their health. And since they have a sense of well-being, they often sleep longer, resulting in better rest!

Psychological Benefits

When we are happy, we definitely experience a whole series of positive emotion which accompany happiness. Bitter people who are always angry, scream on top of their lungs, and blow up over a minor thing are in a state of negativity. When we are negative, life will flow in that direction and everything will come up to continue triggering that feeling. However, if we are grateful and happy, we always feel good. We are composed. We handle problems well.

Experts also tell us that happy people tend to be more active or animated. They can tackle problems easily because they are alert. Inside, the person who is happy feels more pleasure and tends to be more optimistic.

Social Benefits

Happy people love to be with others, and so they tend to be more helpful. They love to share what they have and they feel for the needs and problems of others. In short, they know how to empathize._Because they are grateful, they can easily sense the sadness of people and they often respond with acts of care. In addition, people who are happy find it easy to forgive those who offend them.

Chapter 7:
How to Cultivate Happiness

You and I can cultivate happiness. It's like growing a plant. It begins with a tiny seed that you bury under the dirt and you water for a few days. And before you know it, you have a miniscule seedling trying to push its way up and reaching out to the sun.

There are things you must do to cultivate happiness. No, they are not dependent on what you acquire, but on what you must maintain inside your core being. They relate to what you think and your attitude. We have five rules on how to cultivate happiness.

Rule 1: No Comparing

To cultivate happiness and let it grow, avoid comparing yourself to others. Don't focus on other people's abilities and their wealth. Don't fret if the Smiths have a larger home or that Mr. Smith earns more than you do as shown by their possession of two luxury cars, frequent vacations, and frequent parties at their mansion. Comparing yourself with others make you think less of yourself. Most of all, it brings discouragement. As a result, you would sulk at how unfair the world is toward you. This kills joy.

It is a crime to be preoccupied at comparing who we are with others. They are good-looking and we are not. Our friends are trim and fit, and we have bulging tummies and large arms. Your office mate has six-pack abs but all you have is a mound under your shirt. And you despair, and as a result you deprive yourself of happiness. Don't compare, but simply accept who you are and love yourself. That's the way to cultivate happiness.

Rule 2: No to Perfectionism

One of the so-called joy-stealers is people's tendency to set very high standards for everything. Perfectionism is part of our bad character or personality. We set standards that are unattainable. Perfectionism says you are not allowed to make mistakes. Your work should be error-free, your speech should be refined always, and your writing impeccable. You should be admirable all the time, always performing noble tasks, and never steering away from your set goals. Mind you, no one can live like this. No wonder many of us are so unhappy. Accept yourself and others. Admit that you are not perfect and that you and others are bound to make mistakes. This is how you must think to cultivate happiness inside of you.

Rule 3: No to People-pleasing

Being a people-person is an excellent skill and extremely important in relationships and functioning in society. People-pleasing is different – you do all things possible so that you don't offend anybody. In short, you live according to the expectations of people, and not what is right or what you think is appropriate. When you live like this, you're not living at all. This is utter slavery and this hinders you from cultivating happiness.

Rule 4: No to Distraction

Some of the most fulfilled people I know are those who know who they are. They appreciate their strengths and they are cautious at the same time because they know their weaknesses. They know where to place themselves. These kinds of people also know their priorities and are guided by them, not by people or circumstances. We are not saying that you should be rigid. Our only point is that you must know your focus. People who are focused do not allow the chaos around them to ruin their flow or progression, but they know how to dodge the flying balls and avoid the humps on the road. Avoid distraction to cultivate happiness.

Rule 5: No to Over-commitment

Busyness, workaholic tendency, and refusing to give yourself a break transforms the human into a machine. When you don't find time to breathe and relax, you hurt yourself, as well as the people around you, in the process. Don't overwork yourself thinking that the world will not be the same if you slowed down. All your tasks cannot be completed in a day anyway.

Also, leave work-related problems behind. Don't bring them home and address them while eating dinner or while lying in bed. Learn to say no to extra tasks when you know you have a lot on your plate. Learn to refuse when you have to. This is how to cultivate happiness.

Chapter 8:
The Most Powerful Happiness Habits

Habits are things that we acquire over time due to repeated acts. You can develop happiness habits and your life will never be the same again. There are three powerful habits that must be part of your life.

Worry Less

Work, family life, societal problems, personal concerns – all these are encountered on a regular basis. If we are not careful enough, we end up being overwhelmed by them. And the usual result is worry. We are anxious about the deadlines set, or the problem with a spouse or a child. How do we worry less? It's simple. It's accepting the fact that problems are part of life. All we can do at worrisome times is live with them. In this thing called life, it's a matter of sink or swim. Let problems worry about themselves and we focus on more important things.

Manage Stress

Stress is related to worry. When we worry too much, it results in stress. Stress happens when we have too much on our plate, when we're rushing, scrambling for those deadlines, and projects that must be finished. It's trying to live like a superhero; like Superman. This is simply impossible. We have limits. Let's learn to slow down and swallow only what we can chew. Learn to say no to overwhelming commitments. Don't accept a responsibility that you can't handle well.

Fear Less

Fear is debilitating. It paralyzes us. Fear happens when we don't believe, when we see the waves rather than the safe ground, when we see the problem rather than the solution, when we see death rather than paradise. Fear is the absence of faith and confidence. We fear separation, criticism, failure, rejection, sickness, and death. These are fear-causing scenarios, but you must develop the habit of not being overwhelmed by them. The absence of fear is true freedom and happiness.

Chapter 9:
Exploring Various Faith-based Perspectives On Happiness

Health experts have established that there is a strong connection between wellness, well-being, positive emotions and spirituality. Wellness and positive feelings are actually what bring wholeness, strength, and ecstatic feelings in people. In this section, we would like you to consider some insights on the role of spirituality in experiencing genuine happiness and then take a look at interesting religious perspectives on the religion-happiness connection.

Spirituality and Happiness

Spirituality is central to achieving true happiness and cannot be divorced from religion. Researchers Ed Diener and his son Robert Biswas-Diener have found that spirituality is indeed connected to happiness. In their book entitled 'Happiness: Unlocking the Mysteries of Psychological Wealth', they concluded that people tend to experience a sense of well-being or wholeness from being spiritually connected. They found, among many other conclusions, that spirituality provides psychological comfort for people struggling with issues of death and questions about afterlife.

Involvement in some religious activities also gives a sense of belonging and meaning in life. When one is religious, their belief can provide meaning and a sense of belonging. The 'father and son' tandem explains that religious people are happy because they experience emotions like compassion which speaks of sacrifice and altruism, and forgiveness or the willingness to let a person off the hook for the wrong they have done. These, together with a sense of awe and gratitude, can be made possible because of a person's involvement in religion.

Happiness is a key subject among the world's major religions. You will notice that although people come from various faiths, happiness is as relevant and central as life itself all across cultures and faiths. Indeed, to be happy is everyone's quest in life, as well as afterlife.

Nirvana is Real Happiness

The key to happiness in Buddhist thought is self-denial and separation from the things of the world. To be truly happy, one must detach himself or herself from needs, wants, and other worldly desires. The preoccupation with the material world causes enormous and endless suffering, thus the absence of happiness. Buddhism teaches that when we are able to set aside 'the self' or achieve a state of 'non-being' by freeing the mind, we experience peace of mind also known as mental equanimity. It is at this state wherein Buddhists experience what they call a "transcendent bliss and well-being" (The Pursuit of Happiness, 2016). Buddhism's idea of happiness is contrary to what many consider it to be. In fact, the Buddhist experiences happiness not by having or possessing, not by acquiring and accumulating riches – no, it's not through consumerism or materialism, but by emptying the mind and experiencing nothingness.

Therefore, to be happy in Buddhist religion is to abandon worldly desire and passions. Buddha's portrayal as always smiling was a result not of satisfaction from material things or riches but from tranquility within his very core. In fact, the philosopher had abandoned royalty and riches and lived a life of poverty, of nothingness, and later concluded that true happiness is only possible through renunciation as mind dysfunction or suffering is avoided. The absence of dysfunction happens as an individual learns to focus on the present while not dwelling on the past or the future. Said differently, if we choose the world and what it offers, we suffer and would be deprived of fulfillment, but if we choose abandonment and self-denial, we achieve real happiness.

The third and fourth noble truths of Buddhism indicate that happiness and contentment are attainable so long as people give up their cravings. To be happy, one must also choose to endure pain, while at the same time not allowing fear, hatred and anger to dominate life. This state, characterized by freedom from physical and psychological suffering, is called nirvana, "an experience of profound happiness." An important tool that leads to nirvana is meditation, which trains the mind to focus on the present, and transcends to the unknown, into space, into nothingness.

Happiness in Buddhism is also connected to wisdom, ethical conduct, and mental cultivation. Adherents are taught three categories of wisdom; right speech, right action, and right livelihood which constitute ethical conduct while right effort, right mindfulness, and right concentration represent mental cultivation.

A very important Buddhist practice is the right effort of avoiding and clearing one's mind of any thoughts that are unwholesome or negative. It is through this concentration and pre-occupation on the positive which permeates the inner self with a true sense of tranquility. This state of mind then prepares the way for developing mindfulness and concentration. A very important Buddhist concept, mindfulness, points the individual to the here and now. It is a choice to focus on the present and enjoy it while doing away with the things of the past and not worrying of what is ahead.

In short, happiness is simply the celebration of life and all that is in it whether good or bad.

Happiness is Communion with God

Christianity also emphasizes self-denial and abandonment. This is the path of blessedness or happiness. In Catholicism, for instance, devotion to God, as seen in seclusion and dedication of self to service, and acts of charity are important teachings and practices. While Buddhism talks about emptying oneself to attain nirvana, Christianity emphasizes abandoning the "old nature" or giving up sinful acts and desires and living according to God's will. In this view, emptying oneself is not an end to itself, but the beginning because one must acknowledge his or her need for a relationship with God through faith in Jesus Christ.

In every person's life, so Christianity teaches, is a vacuum that only God can fill. Therefore, without God in one's life, there can be no true happiness. As Augustine wrote, "Thou (You) hast made us for thyself (yourself), O Lord, and our heart is restless until it finds its rest in thee (you)." Ultimately, this means that one should allow God to control one's life and must manifest via constant practice of God's presence. It is a life of communion with God through prayers and study of the Holy Scriptures, which are seen as a moral compass for living.

Christianity's synonymous words for happiness are 'joy', 'rejoice', and 'blessed'. Just like in Buddhist traditions, joy in Christian perspective is not dependent on possessing or achieving something. Christians go further and hold on to faith so that they experience joy amidst trials and sufferings. It is through faith that they see the unseen and are assured of the things they hope for in their present life and after death.

One man who was asked about his definition of happiness gave instead this song that he used to sing in church when he was young. It says,

> *Happiness* is to know the Savior
> Living a life within His favor
> Having a change in my behavior
> *Happiness* is the Lord
>
> *Happiness* is a new creation
> Jesus in me in close relation
> Having a part in His salvation
> *Happiness* is the Lord
>
> Real joy is mine
> No matter if teardrops start,
> I've found the secret--
> It's Jesus in my heart!
>
> *Happiness* is to be forgiven
> Living the life that's worth living
> Taking a trip that leads to heaven
> *Happiness* is the Lord...

Based on the song, happiness is faith in God. It is having a deep relationship with him, resulting in a changed life, hope and an assurance of living in heaven someday.

Happiness is Having Wisdom

Judaism shares with both Buddhism and Christianity the value of self-denial and of wisdom in order to experience joyful living. This kind of wisdom is manifested through right living – called holiness by both Jews and Christians and mental equanimity by Buddhists.

Judaism's Old Testament book of Proverbs declares, "Happy is the man that finds wisdom, and the man that gets understanding" (Prov. 3:13). It also says, "Where there is no revelation, people cast off restraint; but blessed is the one who heeds wisdom's instruction" (Prov. 29:18). In Judaism, right living or being wise is the key to genuine happiness.

Judaism's favorite royalty, King David, wrote an entire psalm on happiness. Using the word blessed or happy, the famous king believes that a person can be happy only if and when he or she avoids wickedness and delights in the law of God. He went on to equate the life of a truly happy person with that of a tree planted by the streams of water - its leaves are always verdant and never dry, and bears lots of fruits in season. He culminated his psalm with a declaration that whatever this person does truly prospers. In Judaism, living right means keeping the law or the Torah, and that would mean success, which brings happiness.

Following the Torah (Judaism's scriptures) which prescribes religious ceremonies for various aspects of life is central to Judaism. For them this is the path to happiness.

Happiness is Paradise on Earth

Followers of Islam appear to have similarities with Judaism and Christianity when it comes to the pursuit of joy. According to Muslim teachings, obedience to God and being part of the true religion, which they believe is Islam, are what will bring true happiness, and not material things. Christianity calls this devotion and holiness while Judaism refers to this as right living or wisdom. Islam teaches that when men and women follow the way of God, they will experience paradise here on earth, and this is what constitutes genuine happiness.

32

God, according to Islamic teachings, rewards those who do right, and this is in a form of a good life. This entails that those who do not follow the teaching will endure a life of suffering. In addition, to be truly happy, one needs to know his or her purpose in life and work towards their entry into paradise or "success in the hereafter."

Islam also emphasizes the value of nurturing not only of the physical body, but also of the heart and soul. Similar to Christianity and Judaism, Islam also teaches that no greater joy can be found outside of God. To be truly happy, one must submit to God, strive to please God every day, and strive to "enter paradise" among others (Demashqeyyah, N.D.).

It appears that spirituality is equated if not a means to enter into physical and spiritual rest (peace of mind in Buddhism and wholeness in Christianity). As in the case of the four major religions mentioned, involvement in religion plays a critical role in experiencing happiness.

Chapter 10:
Buying Experiences Not Possession Leads to Greater Happiness

Possessions do cause one to have a temporary sense of excitement, security and fulfillment. However, happiness is not about having, but being. You will agree with us that we don't have unlimited access to the all the things we desire. And even if we did, we all know that they do not always satisfy on a deep level. Sooner or later, we lose interest and our bodies and our minds crave for more, that is, if our standard of happiness is limited to having material things.

Let's focus on experiences rather than on possessions. They say great gifts come in small packages, and that's true in real life and in our pursuit of happiness. In the same way, life offers countless gifts that are often ignored or taken for granted.

Engaging in Sports

Instead of buying new appliances and extra gadgets that you don't actually need, why not invest in sports? Buy a good basketball and play with your friends. Get yourself a nice pair of running shoes for a morning jog. Invest in things you can share with others and will last a long time.

Having Hobbies

Collect stamps, coins or cards with your friend or a child. You will find it inexpensive, amusing and relaxing. Have time for things you enjoy. Maybe you love plants so you could try gardening. Hobbies not only give you time to unwind but also help you forget the worries of life.

Outings, Bonding Times, Picnics

Being with loved ones, family, or friends gives us a happy feeling. Scrooge from the famous Christmas fairy tale was anti-social and hated celebration especially that of Christmas, only to realize later on how much he had missed. We too miss a lot when we forego outings, bonding times with family, and invitations to weekend picnics. These are special times – a time to unwind, to bond with others, and enjoy relationships.

Biking or a Walk in the Park

Get your bike and let those wheels roll again. Enjoy the breeze while burning some calories as you pedal. Walk in the park on a lazy afternoon or a breezy morning, alone or with some friends or family. Go for the experience and you will find out that life has a lot to offer. Pay attention to the details on the way.

Back Rub or Foot Spa

Go for a foot spa and let your feet be relieved while reading your favorite book. Have your spouse or friend give you a back rub. It is not only relaxing for you, but rewarding for the one rendering you the service.

Singing a Song, Reading a Book

Let out those stresses and belt out your favorite song, in front of a karaoke machine or in the bathroom. Sing with family or friends, even if you're out of tune. You can also grab your favorite novel and travel in time and places, meeting unusual characters, and interacting with the author's arguments and lessons. These are wonderful experiences you should not miss.

All these experiences have the capacity to make life meaningful. They do not require much investment, and if you will be able to stay present in all these activities, you can achieve a great sense of fulfillment and happiness.

Chapter 11:
The Science of Gratitude

Whitney Houston popularized a song entitled "Greatest Love of All." The song goes, "Learning to love yourself, it is the greatest love of all... It's easy to achieve..."

The song implies that there are so many things in us and about us that we must celebrate. Celebrating what we are and who we are is a manifestation of gratefulness. Unfortunately, many people would rather choose to complain about what they do not have that others do.

Gratitude begins in the mind. It's about proper perspective. How come many end up resorting to drugs and alcohol? They disconnect from themselves and lose touch of what there is to be grateful for.

They focus more on media, fashion and models and convince themselves that they ought to look like those models. We should focus and celebrate who we are as people, and the beautiful natural world around us – full of animals, plants, mountains, oceans and so much more! The world is so abundant and there is so much to be grateful for.

Gratitude For Who You Are

Life is more than just what meets our five senses. Who you are is a gift, and your life is no accident. You have your own place under the sun and you have a purpose. You were born to experience joy as you live according to your purpose.

Your value does not lie solely in the things you have collected, but your inner self, your core, the real you. You are able to work, support your family, and take action to make the world a better place.

You may be taller than most people, but you don't have allergies or high blood pressure. You may be short, but you run fast, and work efficiently. Celebrate yourself and be happy! You are who you are!

Gratitude for Your Skills and Strengths

You should be thankful for the skills and talents you accumulated through your life. You can use those skills to contribute to the world and create something beautiful, which will give you a sense of fulfillment once you see the result of your efforts.

Let us show you some examples.

You're a good planner or an expert in strategizing. Amidst the chaos and uncertainties, you're able to come up with instant solutions. You're a good leader and your co-workers respect you. People are inspired by you and are pleased with what you do. You deliver good projects and are always on time, and you can produce a complicated report or develop a business plan in no time.

No one can handle the syringe properly and extract blood without any trouble like you do. Patients can rely on you for you can tell them what's wrong with their bodies. People have houses and cities have buildings and bridges because of your expertise.

You mold young lives and prepare them as the country's future leaders with your teachings. Week after week, you deliver inspiring and life-changing lessons that change lives.

You make your husband and your children happy with your savory meals and well-kept home. You provide warmth to your home, and a sense of comfort and happiness for your family.

You direct people to the right direction on a busy intersection to make sure everyone's safe. Criminals are apprehended and your city is a better place to live because of your contribution.

You serve orders with smile and excellent customer service. You unload bricks, cement, and steel bars with all your might and diligence.

Besides these, you've accomplished so much. Celebrate your successes and accomplishments, your awards and rewards, the appreciation from others you receive, etc.

We can go on and on. You see, you have something that is so important and special that only you can do. Be grateful for all the skills and strengths that have been given to you. Be happy because you have been given opportunities to develop yourself and be of service to others; we are here to support each other!

Gratitude Despite the Odds

In life, not everything is rosy all the time. In fact, many of the things we experience can be unpleasant. Still, we can choose to see the glass half full and view life optimistically while embracing those unpleasant experiences.

Let us imagine a fictional scenario about an imaginary person. This person failed at their job interview, their spouse didn't like their gift, and their children ignored them after coming from school. This imaginary person's teen-aged son is also being rebellious, their close relative is sick, there are bills to pay and those owed are contemplating on suing.

Remember what we said? Do not let circumstances control you and dictate how you must live. Someone has aptly said, *we can't control a bird dropping falling onto our heads, but it is stupidity to let the same bird build a nest in our hair.*

There is always a good side to things. Hope is waiting to be tapped. Failed the interview? There are other jobs waiting for you; it's their loss if they didn't hire you.

Hurt by your kids? They appreciated your cooking last Saturday and they will appreciate you for raising them when they are older too. Focus on the big picture, not what they failed to do today.

Problem child? You teenager is growing up and he just doesn't understand himself yet.

Sick relative? Nobody lives healthy forever, it's a natural cycle of life. Be happy because insurance is covering all the hospitalization and home care expenses.

Friend, cheer up. Cultivate a happy feeling by renewing that sense of hope. Remember it's your call.

Chapter 12:
Exercise = Happiness

In chapter 9, we talked about worrying less and handling your stress well. One way to deal with stress is exercise. When we engage in exercise, we feel good because the body feels good.

Therefore, if you want to be happy, do not neglect exercise, no matter how busy you are or how demanding life is. If you love yourself, you will work at making yourself happy by engaging in regular physical activities. Exercise has lots of benefits and are explained below.

Sense of Well-being

Observe very active or athletic people and you will see one common denominator – they are happy. They may not be literally smiling or laughing but you can sense by their looks and demeanor that they feel good. They are not sluggish, and are solid and move fluidly. They make you feel comfortable. Why? Because they are content inside. This is caused by a hormone that is released when they exercise – dopamine. This hormone gives a sense of well-being, which in turn make us feel good and happy. Your next goal? Exercise more.

Exercise Changes Moods

People who have resorted to regular exercise report that they had never felt greater. They found that even the simplest forms of exercise have tremendous health benefits not only physically but also psychologically. Because the body is relieved during or as a result of exertion, happy hormones are released, as already stated and this wonderful feeling leads to positive thoughts and actions. Because you feel stronger, you feel more motivated in life, say to be more productive or finish a project, clean the house, wash the car, or mow the lawn.

Stress-Buster

It's true, exercise is a good way to deal with stress. Overworked or tired from rushing to beat deadlines? The answer is exercise. Swim a few laps, run a few kilometers, bike in the park, do some workouts at a nearby park or fitness facility and relieve and strengthen those tensed muscles of yours. As a result, you will feel happier, healthier, and more mobile and stable both physically and emotionally. Therefore, never neglect exercise no matter how busy or tired you are. In fact when you feel like your body is about to say "I've had enough," that's when you really have to find time to do some running or stretching.

Exercise Equals Strength

Nobody likes being hungry because we get easily irritated. Our irritability is not caused by impatience at all, but is connected with low sugar and lack of energy. You see, when we lack energy, we feel miserable. People who do not diet well and move enough are not only sluggish but also suffer from lots of aches and pains aside from weakness. To be energized and active, make it a habit to exercise and maintain a healthy wholesome diet.

Exercise Means More Sleep

Remember those times when you went to sleep tired only to wake up feeling exhausted still? You were wishing that after some sleep, your body would have become rested, but alas, nothing changed. One important solution is exercise. Because your muscles are active and toned, they are ready for rest at bedtime. And you can be sure you will be refreshed and renewed when morning comes because of quality sleep. Experts tell us that those who suffer from insomnia should make it a habit to exercise because it induces sleep.

Exercise Leads to Productivity

Because you feel good due to exercise, you have more energy and motivation which are important ingredients regarding work efficiency and productivity. Individuals who are always tired are often not able to achieve their targets in terms of output. When the body is tired and weary, it just starts shutting down. Take care of your body and you'd be doing yourself a big favor – you'd accomplish more, feel more energetic and of course happy as well.

Chapter 13:
Don't Take Yourself So Seriously!!!

Some of the most miserable people in the world are those who live to work, instead of working to live. They focus on their tasks, rather than the moment and the person they are spending time with. They value the project more than the enjoyment in accomplishing it. They are tough, uptight, and high-strung. Maybe it's their temperament, but they must change or chances are they will die unhappy, and early too.

Life is beautiful and we should make room for less serious matters. How? Let us offer the following:

Make Room for Mistakes

Allow yourself to make mistakes because you're not perfect. If you failed, forgive yourself, accept the error, correct it if you can and move on. There is so much more to life than living in regret and focusing on the past. What is broken cannot be made whole at times. The key is acceptance of oneself. Lack of it robs you of the joy that you deserve.

Crack Jokes

How many people do we see in the streets with sad, long faces? These are people who are not only burdened but have forgotten that they have a beautiful life to live. Learn to smile, and to laugh. You must laugh with those who tell silly stories and you will be happy. Also, learn to crack your own jokes too, no matter how awkward or silly they may sound. Relax, life is not all about work and living within boundaries. This is a good way to unwind and feel good.

Loosen Up

Learn to wear sneakers and jeans, or sandals and shorts instead of slacks and shiny leather shoes all the time. Our value does not depend on how we look, but who we are inside. Loosen your tie or hang your coat for a moment. Use your hands to eat your pizza – lick the ketchup off your finger! Simply enjoy the simple things in life and be happy!

Accept Others

Accept those who are different, those whose skin color or cultural background is not the same as yours. You will find that they are just like you, in fact, you might even learn a lot from them. We often end up frustrated and irritated because others are different or they don't behave the way we expect them. This is not a good way to be because we are all united as one humanity. Everybody is our brother and sister and we must unite and learn from one another. Accept and be accepted, spread love and experience happiness.

Welcome Innocence

Let the children make noises or litter their room. Let them be children. Don't think of them as a burden, or as kids that always mess up the house and force you to be constantly clean after them. Let people be people, and let children be what they are meant to be. You were a child once and your parents allowed you to enjoy and play, so do the same for your kids. Allow things to flow.

Learn to Play

Read a nice book and rest your feet on the snack table or on the sofa. Sing along with the birds outside of your window. Walk barefoot in the park and feel the soil and grass under your feet. Stay longer in the shower, and feel the hot water dripping down your back. These are some little ways of enjoying life and playing!

Pamper Yourself

Munch on your favorite snack once in a while without the guilty feeling. Take a day off from work and just do whatever it is you want to do. Stay longer in bed on Saturday mornings and cuddle with your spouse, animal, kids or pillow!

<u>ENJOY YOUR LIFE!</u>

We are not here to work like machines, or to accumulate tons of digits in our bank accounts. We are here to express love, to be free and feel both the joy and sorrows of life – it's all beautiful because it's the expression of creation. Nature has so much to offer us, and we hold so much information and potential inside ourselves. Focus your attention on the simple and little things in life, and go inside to find the truth. If you want happiness, then stop for a second and realize that you already have happiness – it's just waiting for you to notice it.

Conclusion:
You Can Be Happy, Now and Always

After reading this book, you must have realized that happiness is **such an important part of life** that we should do everything to attain it. People have resorted to many things – both good and bad – to acquire it. Some are successful, but others are not. In their desperation, they chose to throw in the towel in life. The absence of happiness is the absence of meaning, of wholeness, of hope, and of reason to live.

Happiness is your calling. It is something that must be acted upon. Don't wait on other people to cause you your happiness as it may never come this way. Plus, people don't inherently owe you anything and so we cannot expect anything from others.

In the final analysis, **we all must learn to swim in this thing called life** and if we don't, we will sink. There are many along the way who may help, but they have also their own lives to live. They, too, must swim in the waters of life to stay afloat and so you must figure it out on your own as well.

Don't wait for circumstances to change, it may not happen on its own. Change your circumstances as long as they're within your capacity to transform them. Those that can't be changed, simply accept them.

Keep focusing on matters or things that can help your growth, and your forward progress as a human being will cause you **gratitude and happiness**. Again, this speaks of your responsibility in making happiness a reality. Look inside yourself and around you. Your existence calls for a celebration. Nature is abundant with so many wonderful things to be enjoyed. Enjoy the time you have and all the opportunities to do all the things that you love. Enjoy people and being with them.

Make happiness a lifestyle. No, it's more than just smiling or thinking happy thoughts. It's having a resolve to turn every situation into something that will contribute to happiness, and if that does not happen, hold on to your pledge to choose to be fulfilled. In short, choose to be happy every time.

Does this mean there is no room for hurts, pain, and grief? Not at all. **We are humans and we are bound to experience all the elements of life**. Our point is to always remember there is more to your current situation, that you have a life to live, that you have a purpose, and there is always a reason to move forward. You are special! Be happy – the choice is in your hands!

Free Bonus eBook Access:
77 Universal Quotes on Happiness

We really hope you enjoyed reading this book, and we want you to know that **we care about our community and the people in it**. That's why we began our collective called 'Cure For The People'. We love to publish lots of different content on various subjects from health to self-help, and much more. We want to open the minds and hearts of our readers, to spread awareness on important topics and have a good time doing it! However, we cannot do what we love to do... without you! Community is the most important part of this movement, and **we want you** to be a part of it!

We would love for you to interact with us and other like-minded individuals on our social media pages, as well as read more great articles and blogs on various related topics, and even get **free chapters from our other books** – all to be found on our website:

www.cure4people.com

You can also find more of our books and video trailers on Amazon which we know **you will LOVE**, by simply visiting our Amazon Author page:

www.amazon.com/author/cure4people

And one last, final thing...

Like we said earlier, community is the most important element required to continue spreading awesome life-changing information to the world – and so if we want people to discover and learn, we need people to trust us and our books! If you could be so kind and helpful, could you please leave us an **honest review** on our Amazon page for this book? We made it super easy and provided the link right here:

www.amazon.com/review/create-review

We give you our big thanks in advance for this super-awesome favor!

As a big 'THANK YOU' we have written a free bonus eBook, *just for you*. It's an eBook that has no availability or access anywhere but <u>right here</u>. As an even bigger bonus, when you download the free book, you will be subscribed to our newsletter which will continue to provide you **additional**

valuable content on this particular subject. We want to continue supporting our readers by engaging with them after they read our books and this is the perfect way to stay connected.

So.. for the moment we have all been waiting for... We present to you... your free bonus ebook:

"77 Universal Quotes on Happiness"

www.cure4people.com/gift-of-happiness-bonus-149

We hope you enjoy this free content, and we wish to continue our relationship through our newsletter, social media channels, website and blog.

Best Wishes from the Cure For The People family!